I CAN BE A
BEAUTICIAN

By Dee Lillegard

Prepared under the direction of Robert Hillerich, Ph.D.

CHILDRENS PRESS®

CHICAGO

Library of Congress Cataloging in Publication Data
Lillegard, Dee.

I can be a beautician.

Includes index.
Summary: Discusses the work of beauticians who take
care of our hair and nails and make us feel good about
ourselves.
1. Beauty operators—Vocational guidance—Juvenile
literature. [1. Beauty culture. 2. Occupations] I. Title.
TT958.L55 1987   646.7'26   87-13835
ISBN 0-516-01910-4

Childrens Press®, Chicago
Copyright ©1987 by Regensteiner Publishing Enterprises, Inc.
All rights reserved. Published simultaneously in Canada.
Printed in the United States of America.
' 2 3 4 5 6 7 8 9 10 R 96 95 94 93 92 91 90 89 88

For Charmaine

PICTURE DICTIONARY

salon

beautician   **hairdresser**

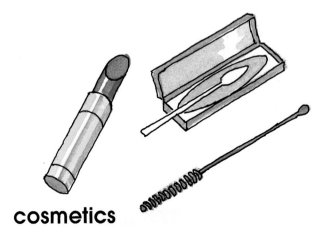

cosmetics

makeup artist

tools

wigs

helper

manicure   **pedicure**

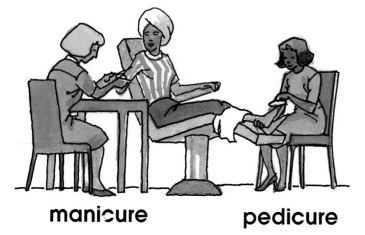

Men and women of all ages
go to beauticians.

beautician

hairdresser

Imagine being an artist—not working with clay or on canvas—but working on people.

Beauticians are artists who work with people. They make people look more beautiful—or more interesting.

Beauticians are also called hairdressers. Most beauticians cut and style hair.

Cosmetologists learn how to put makeup on people.

cosmetics

But many beauticians are cosmetologists. They work on faces, too. The cosmetics they use are like the paints that an artist uses. Makeup, such as lipstick and eye shadow, is used to make a person look better.

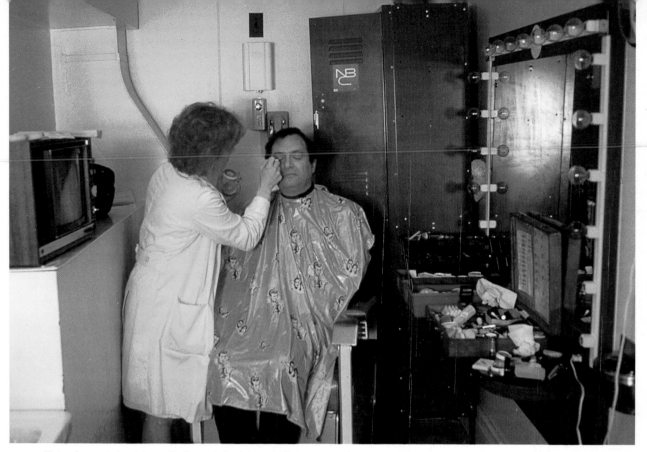

This cosmetologist works for a television station.

These makeup artists can make small eyes look larger. They can make a large nose look smaller. They can even seem to change the shape of a face.

makeup artist

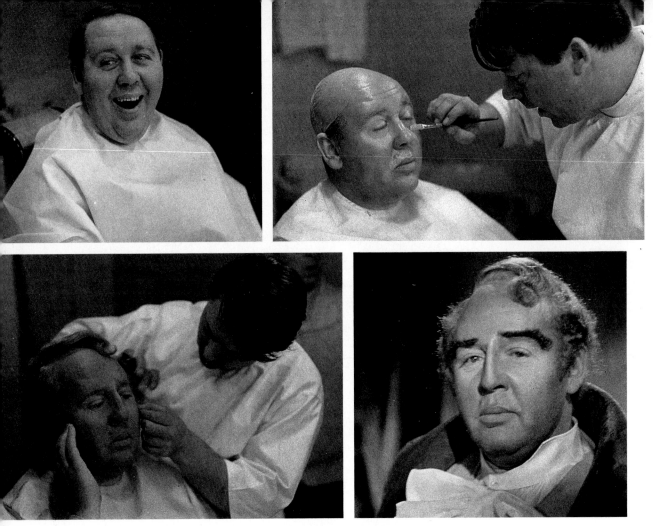

A Hollywood makeup artist used a fake nose made of wax (bottom left), makeup, and a wig to make Charles Laughton (top left) look like a country gentleman who lived in the 1700s.

Makeup artists in television and movie studios can make people look beautiful—or not so beautiful!

Hair stylists use chemicals and curlers to make straight hair curly.

Some beauticians work only on hair. Hair stylists can change the way a person looks. They can curl straight hair or straighten curly hair. And they can give a person's hair a different shape or color.

In the 1700s rich people in France had their hairdressers give them fancy hairdos to go with their fancy clothes.

wigs

Hairdressing was popular in the Middle Ages. Lords and ladies in Europe wore fancy hair styles. In the 1800s, wigs became popular.

Hairdresser
styles a wig.

Hairdressers were needed
to style and clean them.
Today, we also have
hairdressers who work
only on wigs.

A good haircut is important.

Most beauticians work very closely with people. They must have a pleasing voice and good manners. Once in a while, a customer may be rude. But a beautician must always be polite.

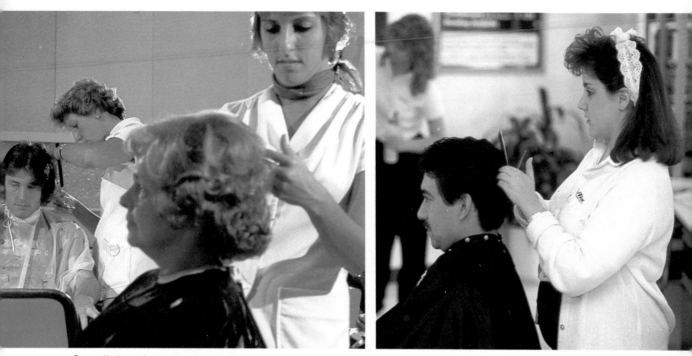

Beauticians learn to style hair
for men as well as women.

Beauticians should
always be clean and
healthy, too. Their
personal appearance
should be a good
example to others.

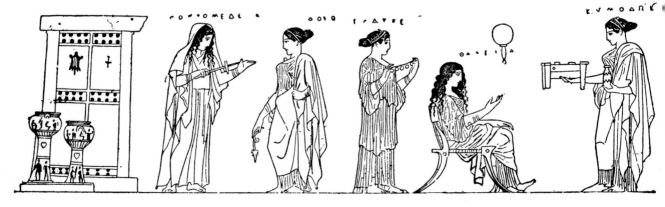

Hair styles worn in Greece thousands of years ago

In ancient Greece, beauty culture was a part of medicine. The Greeks believed that good health and beauty went together.

This is true today, too. A good diet gives you clear eyes, shiny hair, and healthy skin. Using makeup or

Beauticians tell their customers
how to take care of their hair.

having dyed hair cannot
hide an unhealthy body.

Beauticians must like to
work with their hands.
And they must be able to
stand on their feet most of
the working day.

Washing hair and answering the telephone
are some of the jobs in the beauty salon.

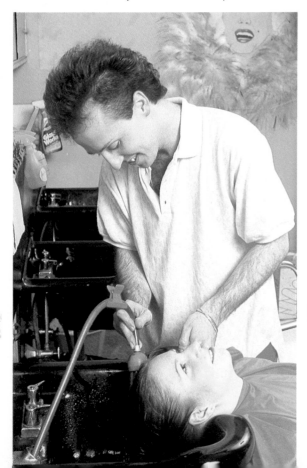

salon

Some beauticians start out as helpers in beauty shops or salons. They sweep the floors and clean all the combs, brushes, and hair curlers.

helper

They may wash customers' hair. They may also help by answering the telephone and making appointments.

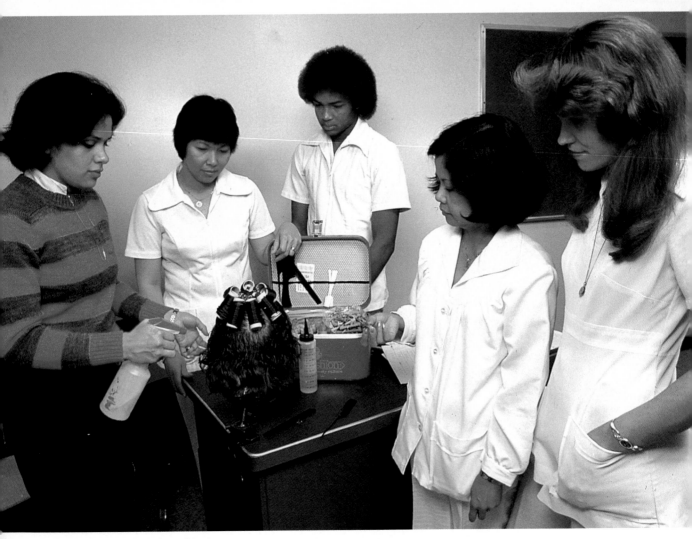

Students learn how to set hair.

There are many things
a beautician needs to
know. Beauticians go to
beauty (or cosmetology)
school to study. All

beauticians must pass a state test to receive a license to work. The tests are different from state to state.

At school beauticians study chemistry and the systems of the body. It is important for them to know the muscles and bones of the head and face.

Students learn how to cut different kinds of hair.

Beauticians learn a lot
about the skin,
particularly the scalp.
They learn about different
kinds of hair. They must be
able to work with all
kinds—hair that is coarse
or fine, soft or wiry.

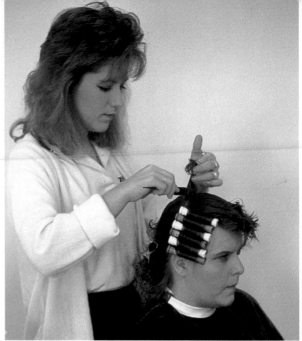

Students learn how to dye hair and give permanents.

Beauticians learn the right way to wash, cut, and style hair. They learn how to give permanents and change the color of a person's hair in a safe way. They also learn how to make damaged hair healthy again.

Rollers, combs, brushes, curling irons, scissors, and hair dryers are the beautician's tools.

Hairdressers use many kinds of brushes and combs, rollers, and hair pins. They must always keep their tools clean. They must also know how to use hair dryers properly.

tools

Beauticians learn how to give manicures.

manicure

Beauticians learn how to make hands beautiful. Some beauticians specialize in *manicures.* They file, shape, and polish fingernails.

24

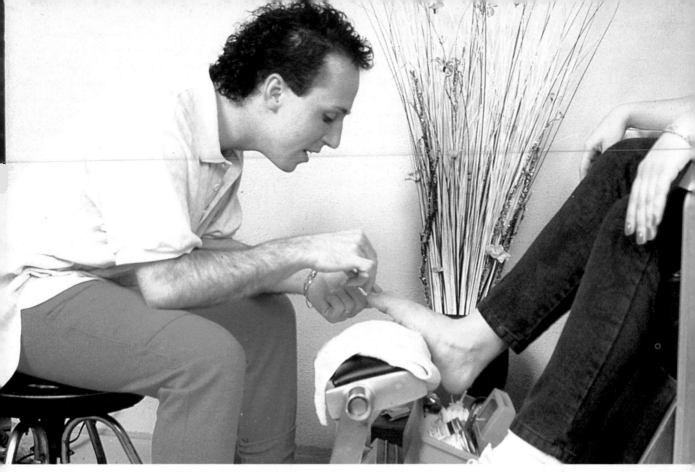

Some beauticians learn how to give pedicures.

Sometimes they apply artificial fingernails.

Some beauticians learn how to work on toenails, too. A beautician who works on people's feet gives *pedicures*.

pedicure

25

A busy beauty shop in Toronto, Canada

Most beauticians work
in salons. Some own their
own businesses or
become salon managers.
There are beauty salons

everywhere—in department stores, hotels. . .even on ships!

Beauticians may have to work nights or weekends. Most shops stay open at these times for customers who work weekdays.

Beauty is not only a science and an art, it's big business as well.

Beauty shops are friendly places.

Some beauticians go
on to teach beauty
culture or write about
beauty and fashion.
Others enjoy selling
beauty products.

Beauticians are very

A successful beautician has many customers.

important to the people they serve. They know the current fashions and styles. Best of all, they know what makes their customers look—and feel—good!

WORDS YOU SHOULD KNOW

appointment (ah • POYNT • ment)—arrangement made for an agreed time with a particular person

art (ART)—a skill at which one succeeds according to one's talent, study, and experience

artificial (ar • tih • FISH • il)—not real, not natural

beautician (byoo • TISH • in)—a person skilled in hairdressing and makeup

canvas (KAN • vis)—a firm, heavy cotton or linen-type cloth used for paintings

coarse (KORSE)—thick, rough; not fine

cosmetics (kahz • MET • ix)—products, as face powder, cream, or lotions, to improve one's appearance or complexion

cosmetologist (kahz • mih • TAHL • ih • jist)—one who studies cosmetics and hair

current (KER • int)—at present, now

dyed (DYED)—changed color of hair

fashion (FASH • un)—the style in dress or manners favored by people

license (LY • cense)—a certificate awarded after a beautician passes tests to prove ability and knowledge of cosmetology

manager (MAN • ih • jer)—person in charge of running a business, or a part of it

manicure (MAN • ih • kyoor)—care of hands and fingernails, by cleansing, massaging, shaping, polishing

pedicure (PED • ih • kyoor)—a cosmetic care of feet and toenails

salons (sal • AWNZ)—a French word meaning a large room for guests; often used to refer to a shop where special products or services are offered; a beauty salon

scalp (SKALP)—the skin on the head

wiry (WHY • ree)—like wire; thin but stiff

INDEX

PHOTO CREDITS

ABOUT THE AUTHOR

Dee Lillegard (Deanna Quintel) is the author of *September To September, Poems For All Year Round,* a teacher resource. She has written several biographies in the Encyclopedia of Presidents recently published by Childrens Press, and many other I CAN BE titles. Over two hundred of Ms. Lillegard's stories, poems, and puzzles have appeared in numerous children's magazines. Ms. Lillegard lives in the San Francisco Bay Area, where she teaches Writing for Children.